Giant Pandas
Up Close

Carmen Bredeson

E Enslow Elementary

CONTENTS

WORDS TO KNOW

bamboo—A plant with tall stems.

China—A country in eastern Asia.

explore (ek SPLOR)—To go into a new place; to look for new things.

snow leopard (LEH purd)—A large, spotted cat that lives in the wild.

Parts of a Panda

head

eye

ear

nose

mouth

fur

body

leg

tail

paw

claw

foot

GIANT PANDA

Imagine a 200-pound teddy bear.
That is what a giant panda looks like!

PANDA HEAD

A giant panda has a big, round head. Its fur is black and white.

Most giant pandas live alone in the mountains of China. A few pandas live in zoos.

PANDA TEETH

UP CLOSE

A panda has big back teeth and a strong jaw.
It chews, chews, chews all day.

The bamboo plant is the panda's favorite food.
A panda eats 25 to 40 pounds of bamboo a day!

PANDA PAWS AND CLAWS

UP CLOSE

Giant pandas walk in the forest on big furry paws.

Each paw has five toes and five sharp claws.

Claws help the panda climb trees.

PANDA "THUMBS"

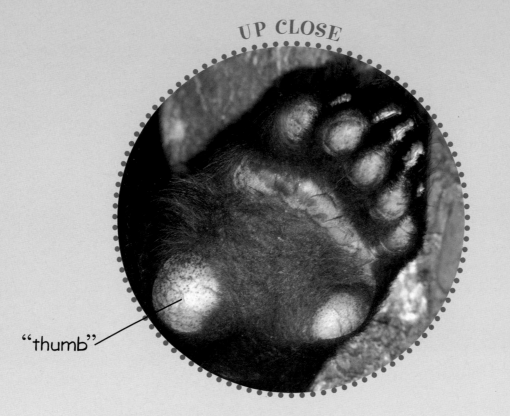

"thumb"

Pandas have something that other bears
do not. Their front paws have a kind of thumb.
The "thumbs" help hold bamboo while the
panda eats.

PANDA EYES

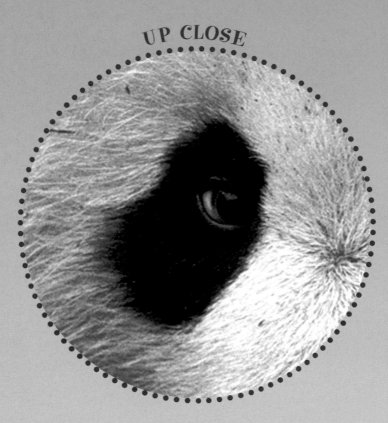

When pandas get tired, their big eyes begin to close. Some pandas crawl into hollow trees to sleep. Others lie down on the ground for the night. Sometimes, pandas nap in trees!

PANDA BABY

new baby
panda

A new baby panda is pink. It is called a
cub. It is about the size of a small banana.
The mother holds it all the time. She keeps
the cub warm and safe in her thick fur.

growing panda cub ▶

PANDA ENEMIES

UP CLOSE

Soon the panda cub starts to crawl around and explore. The mother teaches her cub for two years.

She guards her baby from snow leopards, wild dogs, and black bears. These animals might try to eat the little panda.

Mother and cub ▶
hide in a tree.

SAVING PANDAS

There are only about 1,600 giant pandas left in the world. Many people are working to save the pandas.

They are trying to save the forests where they live. They are helping pandas have babies in zoos.

Each cub is one more panda for the world to enjoy.

LIFE CYCLE

NEW BABY
One or two babies
are born at a time.

CUB
It takes about 4 to 7
years to grow up.

ADULT
It lives up to 35 years in a zoo.
Scientists don't know how long
they live in the wild.

LEARN MORE

Books

Dolbear, Emily J., and E. Russell Primm. *Pandas Have Cubs*. Minneapolis, Minn.: Compass Point Books, 2001.

Eckart, Edana. *Giant Panda*. New York: Children's Press, 2003.

Stone, Lynn M. *Giant Pandas*. Minneapolis, Minn.: Lerner Publications Co., 2002.

Web Sites

San Diego Zoo. *Mammals: Giant Panda.* <http:www.sandiegozoo.org>.

Click on "Animals & Plants," then "Animal Bytes."
Then click on "Mammal," then "Giant Panda."

Smithsonian National Zoological Park. *Giant Pandas.* <http://nationalzoo.si.edu>.

Click on "Animals, etc.," then "Giant Pandas."

INDEX

Series Literacy Consultant:
Allan A. De Fina, Ph.D.
Past President of the New Jersey Reading Association
Professor, Department of Literacy Education
New Jersey City University
Jersey City, New Jersey

Science Consultant:
Don Lindburg, Ph.D.
Associate Director of Panda Conservation
San Diego Zoo
San Diego, California

Note to Parents and Teachers: The **Zoom In on Animals!** series supports the National Science Education Standards for K–4 science. The Words to Know section introduces subject-specific vocabulary words, including pronunciation and definitions. Early readers may need help with these new words.

For Andrew and Charlie, our wonderful grandsons

Enslow Elementary, an imprint of Enslow Publishers, Inc.

Enslow Elementary® is a registered trademark of Enslow Publishers, Inc.

Library of Congress Cataloging-in-Publication Data

Bredeson, Carmen.
  Giant pandas up close / Carmen Bredeson.
    p. cm. — (Zoom in on animals!)
  Includes index.
  ISBN-10: 0-7660-2496-2 (hardcover)
  1. Giant panda—Juvenile literature. I. Title.
  QL737.C214B74 2006
  599.789—dc22
                              2005003330
  ISBN-13: 978-0-7660-2496-0

Printed in the United States of America

10 9 8 7 6 5 4 3 2

To Our Readers: We have done our best to make sure all Internet Addresses in this book were active and appropriate when we went to press. However, the author and the publisher have no control over and assume no liability for the material available on those Internet sites or on other Web sites they may link to. Any comments or suggestions can be sent by e-mail to comments@enslow.com or to the address on the back cover.

Photo Credits: Keren Su/China Span; Terry Whittaker/ Photo Researchers, Inc., p. 18.

Cover Photos: Keren Su/China Span

Enslow Elementary
an imprint of
Enslow Publishers, Inc.
40 Industrial Road   PO Box 38
Box 398   Aldershot
Berkeley Heights, NJ 07922 Hants GU12 6BP
USA   UK
http://www.enslow.com